OLD WOODY GOES SOWIN

CANDLE BOOKS

At last spring had arrived.
Old Woody got up early to go out to his field.
Filbert the cat went too. Old Woody had to sow his seed.

The sun was just rising. For a few minutes Old Woody simply stood and watched.
Then he got down to work.

Old Woody started to break up the soil with his spade. He soon felt very hot.
While Woody was hard at work, Filbert the cat caught sight of something.
Can you see what interested Filbert so much?

First Old Woody smoothed down the soil with his rake. Then, after filling his bowl with seed, Woody walked up and down the field, scattering handfuls of seed as he went.

Soon the birds were back. They gobbled up as many seeds as they could find.
Woody thought: That's not fair! I've spent all morning sowing the seeds – and now they just gobble them up. *Those* seeds will never grow into fresh, green corn.

Woody chased after the birds, flapping his arms. 'Hey – clear off, you greedy things,' he shouted crossly.

The birds flew off. They were a bit frightened of Old Woody – and very frightened of Filbert the cat.

Suddenly Woody had a bright idea. He made a big doll, nearly as tall as he was, and dressed it in some of his oldest clothes. He had a scarecrow! Old Woody stuck his scarecrow right in the middle of the field.
Now the birds kept well away!

Seeds need plenty of sunshine to grow. And they need water, too.
Woody sprinkled water over the field with his watering-can.

Woody and Filbert the cat worked hard all day. After all this work, they were feeling pretty tired, so they took a break under a shady tree.

Every single day Old Woody went out to see if his seeds were coming up yet. But even after a whole week there was nothing to see. Then, a few days later, Woody saw the very first green shoots springing from the ground.

What a pity! A few of the young shoots shot up very quickly – but then died. They were growing in hard, dry soil. They weren't getting the water they needed.

In some parts of Old Woody's field lots of weeds were growing. The weeds were tall and strong, and took up lots of room. Woody's seeds couldn't grow there – they were all squeezed out by the weeds.

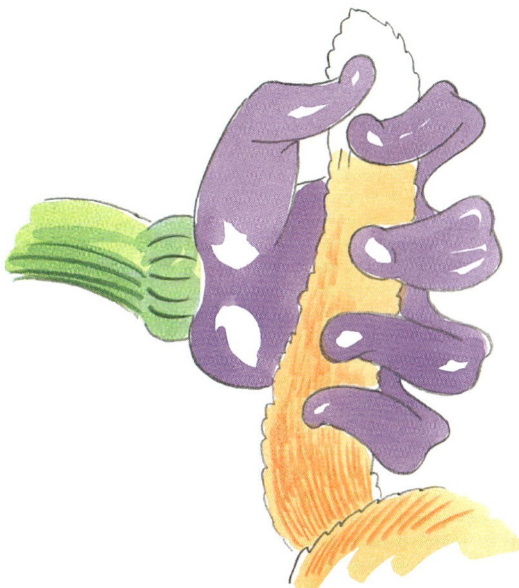

Old Woody tried to pull up the weeds. But even though Filbert helped, he couldn't manage it. The weeds were simply too strong.

Spring went by – and then summer. At last it was harvest-time.
Old Woody set out for his field with a wheel-barrow full of tools. Filbert the cat went too, of course. They were going to cut the corn.

Woody was very happy!
So many rich ears of corn had grown up from the little seeds he had sown. And each ear of corn was full of new seeds.

This story about Old Woody is similar to a story that Jesus told about a sower. You can find it in your Bible in Luke 8:4-15.

Jesus said, 'If we love God and do good, we are like the ears of corn that have lots of seeds.'